*Explore and Learn*

# People in Place and Time

World Book, Inc.
233 N. Michigan Avenue
Chicago, IL 60601
U.S.A.

Volume 1: Earth and Space
Volume 2: Science and Technology
Volume 3: The Natural World
Volume 4: People in Place and Time
Volume 5: Me and My Body
Volume 6: Atlas of the World

For information about other World Book publications, visit our Web site at **http://www.worldbookonline.com** or call **1-800-WORLDBK (967-5325)**.

For information about sales to schools and libraries,
call **1-800-975-3250 (United States); 1-800-837-5365 (Canada)**.

**The Library of Congress has cataloged an earlier edition of this title as follows:**

Explore and learn--people in place and time.
 p. cm.
 Summary: "Introduction to history and world civilizations, using simple text, stories, illustrations, and photos. Features include activities and projects, definitions, review questions, fun facts, school curriculum correlations, and an index"
--Provided by publisher.
 Includes index.
 ISBN 978-0-7166-3020-3
 1. Civilization--History--Juvenile literature. 2. World history--Juvenile literature. I. World Book, Inc. II. Title: People in place and time.
CB69.2.E97 2008
909--dc22
9937                    2008001364

This edition:
ISBN: 978-0-7166-3027-2 (People in Place and Time)
ISBN: 978-0-7166-3023-4 (set)

Printed in China by Shenzhen Donnelley Printing Co., Ltd., Guangdong Province
2nd printing May 2010

Cover acknowledgments:
© Elvele Images/Alamy Images;
© David Peta, Shutterstock

Editor in Chief: Paul A. Kobasa

Supplementary Publications
 Associate Director: Scott Thomas
 Managing Editor: Barbara A. Mayes
 Senior Editor: Kristina Vaicikonis
 Manager, Research: Cheryl Graham

Manager, Contracts & Compliance
(Rights & Permissions):
 Loranne K. Shields

Graphics and Design
 Manager: Tom Evans
 Coordinator, Design Development and Production:
 Brenda B. Tropinski
 Senior Designers: Don Di Sante, Isaiah W. Sheppard, Jr.
 Coordinator: Matt Carrington

Production
 Director, Manufacturing and Pre-Press: Carma Fazio
 Manager, Manufacturing: Steven Hueppchen
 Production Technology Manager: Anne Fritzinger
 Proofreader: Emilie Schrage

Marketing
 Chief Marketing Officer: Patricia Ginnis
 Associate Director: Jennifer Parello

Specialist consultants: Dr. Belinda Ashon; Clive Carpenter; Janet Dyson MEd (education consultant); Tim Furniss (spaceflight journalist and author); Elysa Jacobs; Keith Lye BA, FRGS (geographical author and consultant); Steve Parker BSc (Scientific Fellow of the Zoological Society of London); Peter Riley BSc, Cbiol, MIBiol, PGCE (science writer and consultant); Sue Robson MA, PGCE (Senior Lecturer in education); Carol Watson (children's author)

*Explore and Learn*

# People in Place and Time

Clifton Park - Halfmoon Public Library
475 Moe Road
Clifton Park, New York 12065

volume 4

WORLD
BOOK

a Scott Fetzer company
Chicago
www.worldbookonline.com

# Contents

# All about your book

Explore and Learn will take you on a journey of discovery. Its six volumes will lead you through the world of plants and animals, into science and technology, explaining how things work and why. It will tell you about the world you live in, traveling farther into space and beyond. You can discover new and wonderful things about yourself and how you communicate with those around you.

**Thumb index** This is a guide to what each page contains. If you turn the pages quickly you will easily be able to find the subjects you are interested in.

**Volume button**
This tells you which volume you are looking at. Here is the People in Place and Time button that explores our world.

## exploring

Think, find, research, act out — these boxes help you to discover more about what you have read on a page. See if your family and friends can help you with some of these activities and ideas.

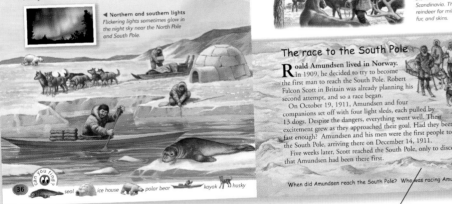

### Lands of ice and snow

The most northerly place in the world is the North Pole. It lies in the middle of the Arctic Ocean, much of which stays frozen solid all year-round. The lands around the ocean are bitterly cold. There are icy mountains and deep-frozen plains, called the tundra. The frozen land around the South Pole is called Antarctica. Nobody lives there, but some scientists work there in special bases. They mainly study the weather. Antarctica is the coldest and windiest place on Earth. Penguins live on the icy coast of Antarctica, and whales swim in the surrounding seas.

◄ **Northern and southern lights**
*Flickering lights sometimes glow in the night sky near the North Pole and South Pole.*

◄ **Amundsen**
*This man was first to reach the South Pole. Read about how he did this in the story below.*

**word search**
**kayak** a type of light canoe, covered with sealskin or canvas.
**reindeer** a deer found in Europe, Asia, and North America. It is sometimes called the caribou.
**tundra** deep-frozen plains where no trees can grow.

◄ **Reindeer herders**
*The Sami people live in the far north of Scandinavia. They keep reindeer for milk, meat, fur, and skins.*

### The race to the South Pole

Roald Amundsen lived in Norway. In 1909, he decided to try to become the first man to reach the South Pole. Robert Falcon Scott in Britain was already planning his second attempt, and so a race began.

On October 19, 1911, Amundsen and four companions set off with four light sleds, each pulled by 13 dogs. Despite the dangers, everything went well. Their excitement grew as they approached their goal. Had they been fast enough? Amundsen and his men were the first people to reach the South Pole, arriving there on December 14, 1911.

Five weeks later, Scott reached the South Pole, only to discover that Amundsen had been there first.

When did Amundsen reach the South Pole? Who was racing Amundsen?

seal    ice house    polar bear    kayak    husky

36    37

where we live

You might choose to read each book from beginning to end, or you might decide to look up things that interest you in the index which appears at the end of each book. All the different features have been created to help you learn, discover, and have fun finding out. You might just enjoy turning each page and looking at all the wonderful pictures showing life and the world around you.

**Stories**
You can find stories that come from different countries all over the world. Some are myths, others are fables, and some are taken from the Bible. How much can you remember? See if you can answer the questions that appear at the end of each story.

**Fun facts** Amazing true facts that will surprise you and your friends.

| English | Math | Science | History | Geography | Art | Music | Design and technology | Information technology |
|---------|------|---------|---------|-----------|-----|-------|----------------------|-----------------------|

**Curriculum buttons** These help you, your parents, and maybe your teacher, to work out which subjects are covered on each page. Do you like history? If so, you can turn the pages and read about history wherever you see this button. Or, maybe you like to draw – watch for this icon. Do you enjoy reading? Watch for the English button.

## Fun characters

Meet our fun characters and their dog. You will find them on our bulletin boards where we put words and pictures for you to learn. You can also find them on the **Fun facts**.

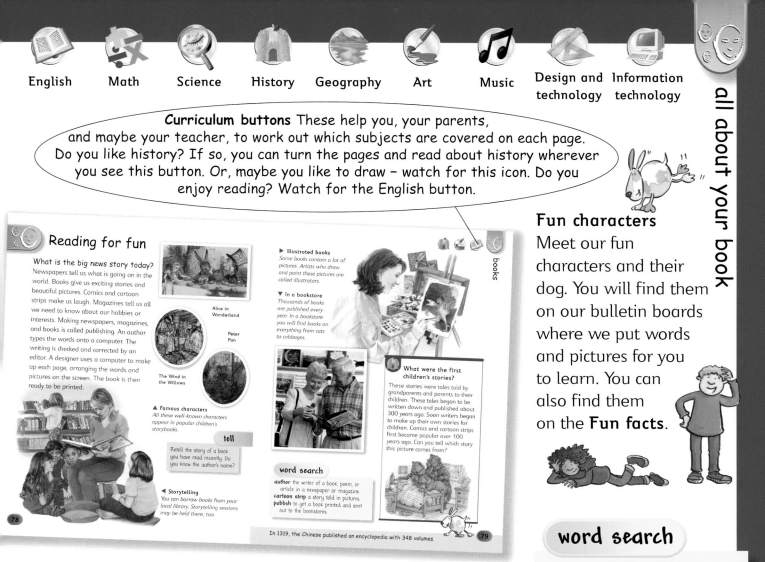

### Reading for fun

What is the big news story today? Newspapers tell us what is going on in the world. Books give us exciting stories and beautiful pictures. Comics and cartoon strips make us laugh. Magazines tell us all we need to know about our hobbies or interests. Making newspapers, magazines, and books is called publishing. An author types the words onto a computer. The writing is checked and corrected by an editor. A designer uses a computer to make up each page, arranging the words and pictures on the screen. The book is then ready to be printed.

Alice in Wonderland

Peter Pan

The Wind in the Willows

▲ **Famous characters**
All these well-known characters appear in popular children's storybooks.

**tell**
Retell the story of a book you have read recently. Do you know the author's name?

◄ **Storytelling**
You can borrow books from your local library. Storytelling sessions may be held there, too.

▶ **Illustrated books**
Some books contain a lot of pictures. Artists who draw and paint these pictures are called illustrators.

▼ **In a bookstore**
Thousands of books are published every year. In a bookstore you will find books on everything from cats to cabbages.

**What were the first children's stories?**
These stories were tales told by grandparents and parents to their children. These tales began to be written down and published about 300 years ago. Soon writers began to make up their own stories for children. Comics and cartoon strips first became popular over 100 years ago. Can you tell which story this picture comes from?

**word search**
**author** the writer of a book, poem, or article in a newspaper or magazine.
**cartoon strip** a story told in pictures.
**publish** to get a book printed and sent out to the bookstores.

In 1319, the Chinese published an encyclopedia with 348 volumes.

books

78

79

### What is the answer?

Do you know? Read on and find out. These boxes will help you learn more about history, geography, science, and other subjects. A **curriculum button** appears at the top beside the question. This tells you what subject is covered. You can choose whatever boxes you are most interested in to read about.

## word search

This will explain and give the meaning of any new or difficult words that are used on a page. You can test yourself to see if you can spell the words or know what they mean. Or, see if you can find where they appear on the page.

### Projects

You can draw, paint, build, and construct all sorts of different things. You will find a list of everything you will need to make each project. Carefully follow the step-by-step instructions that tell you how to make and complete each project. Don't forget to ask an adult for help with some of the more difficult steps.

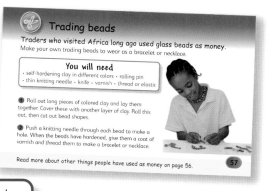

### Trading beads
Traders who visited Africa long ago used glass beads as money. Make your own trading beads to wear as a bracelet or necklace.

**You will need**
· self-hardening clay in different colors · rolling pin
· thin knitting needle · knife · varnish · thread or elastic

❶ Roll out long pieces of colored clay and lay them together. Cover these with another layer of clay. Roll this out, then cut out bead shapes.

❷ Push a knitting needle through each bead to make a hole. When the beads have hardened, give them a coat of varnish and thread them to make a bracelet or necklace.

Read more about other things people have used as money on page 56.

57

Children should be assisted in using certain tools and undertaking particular tasks. Children should not be left unsupervised to carry out these projects.

# Time ticks away

**There are 60 seconds in a minute and 60 minutes in an hour.** There are 24 hours in a day, which is the time it takes the planet Earth to spin around once. There are 365 days in a year, roughly the time it takes the Earth to travel once around the Sun, except for every fourth year when there are 366 days. These are called leap years — February has 29 days instead of 28. How many years old are you? Can you imagine one hundred years? A thousand years? A million? In this book we will travel far back in time to find out how people lived long ago. We will also see how people live on our planet today.

**1** water clock

**2** candle clock

**3** sundial

**4** hourglass

## ▼ Clockwork time
*This pocket watch ran on clockwork. It was made more than 150 years ago.*

## ▲ Telling the time
*Before modern clocks, people invented ways to tell the time.* **1** *Water clocks were used 3,400 years ago. They measured the speed at which water drained out of a pot.* **2** *Candle clocks measured time by burning candles in marked stages.* **3** *Sundials showed shadows as the Sun moved across the sky. The shadows pointed to the time on the dial.* **4** *Hourglasses worked like egg-timers.*

## ▼ Time on Earth

*What time it is depends on where you live in the world.
All these things are happening at the same time.*

the Sun is rising in Alaska and children are eating breakfast

the Sun is high in the sky in Washington, DC, USA, and it's time for lunch at school

the Moon is shining in Beijing, China, and children are fast asleep

it's getting dark in London, UK, and it's time for eating dinner

Alaska
USA

Beijing
China

Washington,
DC, USA

London
England

## Why is history more than learning about dates?

History is the study of past events. It is a way of traveling back through time, discovering the lives of kings and queens, explorers and famous people, and of finding out how people used to live. We are now going to start this journey.

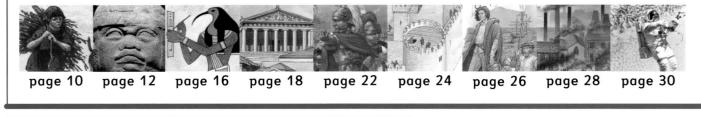

10,000  9000  8000  7000  6000  5000  4000  3000  2000  1000  BC  0  AD  1000  2000

◄ *This timeline tells you the dates in history that are covered on each page.*

# Hunters to settlers

Early Asian people lived by hunting or gathering food. As time moved on, some of them learned how to grow crops and keep animals. Some of the first farmers lived between two great rivers, the Tigris and the Euphrates, in Syria and Mesopotamia (modern-day Iraq). They grew wheat and barley and raised sheep. They made pottery and traded with each other. Soon villages grew into towns, and towns grew into cities. These were the world's first civilizations. They had soldiers, judges, priests, and emperors. Great civilizations later grew up in many other places.

▲ **Life in China**
*Huts like these, in the village of Banpo, were built by farmers in China around 7,000 years ago.*

### ▼ The first writing

It is believed that the Sumerians invented writing about 5,500 years ago, using pictures for words. Later, they pressed shapes into soft clay with sharpened reeds.

### ▲ The city of Ur

About 5,500 to 2,600 years ago, people called Sumerians, Akkadians, and Babylonians ruled the Middle East. They built huge towers called ziggurats. They were like pyramids with stepped sides. This one was in the city of Ur. It was meant to be a home for the Sumerian moon god, who was called Nanna.

### ▼ Inventing the wheel

The Sumerians used wheels to make pottery. By about 5,500 years ago, they were using wheels on carts and chariots.

## word search

**AD** dates that follow the birth of Jesus Christ – about 2,000 years ago.

**BC** dates before the birth of Jesus Christ.

**civilization** a way of life that includes laws, trade, government, arts, and sciences.

**pyramid** a tall building with a square base and four triangle-shaped sides that come to a point at the top.

# Cities of the Sun

**People first came into North America from Asia.** This probably happened at least 15,000 years ago, when these two parts of the world were joined by a strip of land. Over time, humans spread down through North, Central, and South America, following the herds of wild animals that they hunted. The people who settled in Mexico and in the Andes mountains of South America started to grow crops over 10,000 years ago. By about 4,500 years ago, great civilizations were beginning to grow up in these regions. The ruins of great pyramids, temples, and towns can still be seen today.

▼ **The city of Teotihuacán**
*About 1,500 years ago, the Mexican city of Teotihuacán was one of the biggest cities in the world. A huge pyramid was built at its center.*

## ▲ Stone carving

This gigantic stone carving may show a ruler of the Olmec people. It was carved in Mexico about 3,000 years ago.

## ▼ All-American crops

Many crops that are now eaten all over the world were first grown in the Americas.

squash

maize

tomatoes

sweet potatoes

## ▲ Lord of the Maya

This painting was made about 1,300 years ago. It shows the royal court of the Maya in the Mexican rain forest.

## find

Can you find North, Central, and South America in an atlas?

# Seven wonders of the world

**Over 2,100 years ago, there were already tourists.** They traveled around Europe, Southwest Asia, and North Africa to look at great buildings. Some travelers wrote lists of the most incredible sights they had ever seen. These are known as the Seven Wonders of the Ancient World. They have all disappeared, except for the Great Pyramid in Egypt, which is still standing today. Remains of some of the other wonders can be seen in museums.

▲ **Hanging Gardens of Babylon**
*Beautiful gardens were built in ancient Babylon. The gardens rose from the river in huge steps or terraces. They may have been built over 2,600 years ago by King Nebuchadnezzar II for his wife.*

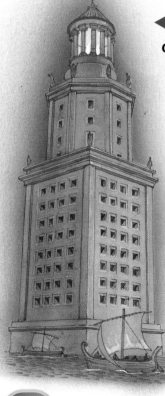

◀ **Pharos Lighthouse at Alexandria**
*The most famous lighthouse ever built stood on an island in the harbor of Alexandria in Egypt. It was as high as 440 feet (135 meters) high. A fire was lit at the top and could be seen far away at sea.*

◀ **Colossus at Rhodes**
*A gigantic statue of the Sun god Helios stood at the entrance to the harbor on the island of Rhodes, Greece. It was more than 107 feet (30 meters) high. It was made of iron and bronze that flashed in the sunlight. The statue was finished around 280 BC, but was later destroyed in an earthquake.*

10,000    9000    8000    7000    6000    5000    4000    3000    2000    1000    BC  0  AD    1000    2000

### ▶ Statue of Zeus at Olympia

*Zeus was the most important god in ancient Greece. A statue of him was built about 2,440 years ago, measuring 39 feet (12 meters) in height. The statue was placed in a beautiful temple, one of the biggest in all of Greece.*

### ▲ Great Pyramid at Giza

*Nearly 2½ million blocks of stone were used to build the Great Pyramid, the largest of the ten built, over 4,500 years ago in Egypt. Thousands of workers labored under the hot Sun. Three huge pyramids are still standing on the edge of the desert, near Cairo.*

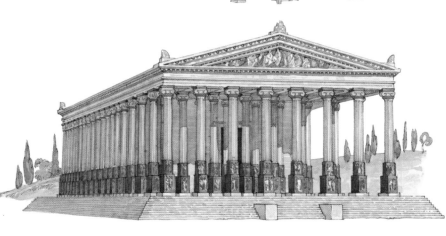

### ▲ Temple of Artemis at Ephesus

*This huge temple was built by a rich king named Croesus about 2,550 years ago in Turkey. It was decorated with fantastic statues made of gold and silver. Someone burned the temple down, so it was rebuilt. In the end, it was destroyed by soldiers during a war. Parts of the temple can still be seen in museums.*

## think

Can you think of Seven Wonders of the Modern World? Look through the pages of this book to help you choose your list.

### ◀ Mausoleum at Halicarnassus

*This huge tomb was built about 2,350 years ago by a Greek queen named Artemisia, in memory of her husband, King Mausolus of Caria. The tomb was destroyed by a series of earthquakes about 900 years ago, but some of its beautiful stone carvings can still be seen in a museum in Turkey.*

# Land of the pharaohs

**The River Nile flows through the hot, dusty deserts of Egypt.** About 8,000 years ago, farmers were planting crops on its muddy banks. By about 3100 BC, the great civilization of ancient Egypt, which lasted for thousands of years, had grown up there. The Egyptians built cities and temples and huge pointed tombs called pyramids. They were the first to make and use paper. Their rulers were called pharaohs. When an important person died, the Egyptians dried out the body and wrapped it in bandages so it would last forever. It was called a mummy. We are still discovering these mummies today.

▶ **Egyptian gods**
*This is Thoth, god of wisdom, one of hundreds of gods and goddesses worshiped by the Egyptians.*

◀ **Face of the mummy**
*Scientists look at mummies to find out how people lived in ancient Egypt — for example, what food they ate and how long they lived. They look at bones, teeth, cloth wrappings, and jewelry.*

## find

Use your atlas to find out which continent Egypt is on.

10,000  9000  8000  7000  6000  5000  4000  3000  2000  1000  BC  0  AD  1000  2000

## How did the ancient Egyptians make paper?

In ancient Egypt, paper was made from papyrus, a kind of reed that grows in the River Nile delta. The ancient Egyptians cut the reeds and stripped off the outer layers. They soaked the insides of the reeds in water and pressed them into strips. They hammered the strips together, dried them, and smoothed them into paper.

papyrus

### ▼ Queen Nefertiti

*Nefertiti was a queen of ancient Egypt. This beautiful statue shows her wearing makeup and a valuable necklace.*

### ◄ The Pyramids

*The Pyramids were built on the edge of the desert. The Great Sphinx is a statue that has a human head and a lion's body.*

## word search

**worshiped** gave thanks and praise to a god or goddess.

### ▼ Picture writing

*From about 3200 BC, the ancient Egyptians used a writing made up of small pictures called hieroglyphs. The writing below spells out the name Cleopatra.*

# The golden age of Greece

Greece is part of southern Europe. It is a land of mountains, islands, and blue seas. Fine palaces were being built on the island of Crete 5,000 years ago. The greatest age of Greece was in 500 to 400 BC. Thinkers, writers, sculptors, architects, and politicians all lived in splendid cities such as Athens and Corinth. Beautiful Greek temples, pottery, and statues built then can still be seen today. Democracy, government according to the wishes of the people rather than by a king or dictator, was first tried in Athens. Only Greek men were allowed to vote for new laws, not women or slaves.

▲ **The city of Athens**
*The Parthenon towered above the beautiful city of Athens, on a hill called the Acropolis. It was a temple to Athena, the goddess of warfare, wisdom, arts, and crafts. The Parthenon was finished in 432 BC. Its ruins still stand today.*

### ▼ The Minotaur

*In ancient Greece there were tales of a monster called the Minotaur. The creature, who was said to live on the island of Crete, was half-bull and half-man.*

### What was the wooden horse of Troy?

Homer, a poet, told how Greek warriors attacked the city of Troy. They could not get into the city, so pretended to go away, but they left a horse made of wood outside the city. The people of Troy were puzzled and dragged the horse inside the city walls. Hidden inside it were soldiers who jumped out and attacked the city.

### ▼ At the theater

*The ancient Greeks liked to go to the theater, to see comedies (funny plays) as well as tragedies (sad plays).*

## word search

**warriors** people who fight in a battle.

# A village from long ago

A thousand years ago, most people didn't live in houses in large cities like most of us do today, but in huts in small villages. Make this model and learn more about the way people lived all this time ago.

To create an earth color, mix brown and a little black and white paint with the plaster.

## You will need

- 2 lb (1 kg) plaster of Paris · construction paper · scissors · tray · tape · twigs and sticks · small box · paints and brushes · soil · straw or dried long grasses · glue · colored modeling clay · colored moss · grass

**1** Make the plaster according to the manufacturer's instructions and pour it over the tray. Shape the plaster into a raised area surrounded by a ditch. Make some paths across the ditch. Push some thick twigs into the plaster for tree trunks, and a line of sticks for fence posts.

## Do people still live like this today?

There are still villages in some parts of the world where people live in a simple way. They grow their own food, keep chickens and pigs, and make everything they need from the trees, plants, and earth around them. They weave baskets and mats and make their own pottery and ironwork.

**2** Make a round house from construction paper. Bend the paper and use tape to form the circular wall, cutting a small hole for the door. Cut out a circular roof; bend it into a cone and fasten it with tape. Stick straw or dried long grasses to the roof. Attach the roof to the top of the house with tape.

**3** Use a small box painted light brown to make the chicken house. Attach sticks to the box with tape to raise it off the ground.

**4** Paint the ground green. Brush glue in areas where you want to stick grass and then sprinkle on the grass. Add soil in front of the hut and along the paths. Make small bushes from colored moss and attach some to the twigs to look like small trees.

**5** Weave green twigs or straw through the posts around the settlement to finish the fencing. Using colored modeling clay, make some pigs and chickens to live in the chicken house.

# The mighty Roman empire

About 1,900 years ago, the Italian city of Rome had fine temples and statues, busy streets, and bustling markets. It was the center of a mighty empire. Roman soldiers marched across Europe, western Asia, and North Africa. They carried iron swords and spears and fought many battles. Wherever the Romans went, they built long, straight roads and fine new towns. They traded in wheat, wine, pottery, and wool. The Romans spoke a language called Latin. They wrote poetry and history books that we still read today.

## word search

**aqueduct** a bridge carrying water across a valley.
**empire** countries controlled by a person or government.

▲ **Julius Caesar**
*Julius Caesar was a brilliant Roman soldier. He became leader in 49 BC but was stabbed to death five years later.*

**▼ Cruel sports**
*The Romans liked to watch cruel sporting displays in which fighters called gladiators killed each other.*

**▲ Pont du Gard**
*This Roman aqueduct can still be seen today in France near Nîmes.*

## describe

Imagine you are a Roman child living in Pompeii. Describe what happened when the volcano Vesuvius erupted.

**▶ Buried by a volcano**
*This was the Roman town of Pompeii. It was buried in ash from Vesuvius, a nearby volcano, in AD 79.*

# New kingdoms and empires

**The Roman empire fell apart after fierce warriors from northern Europe and southwestern Asia began to invade Rome about 1,800 years ago.** There were many wars, and most of Europe was divided up into small kingdoms. There were also powerful new empires. Kings built huge castles that were sometimes attacked by knights in armor. The Christian religion spread through Europe, and people built beautiful churches and cathedrals. Christians and followers of other religions, particularly Muslims, fought against each other in Spain, Portugal, Africa, and the Middle East. European merchants reached China and found a vast empire with great cities. There were also great empires in India, Africa, Mexico, and Peru.

### ▶ The Vikings

*From the late 700s to about 1100, fierce warriors from Scandinavia called Vikings invaded many parts of Europe. They crossed the ocean in longships. Some even reached Greenland and the North American mainland.*

*can you find?*  leather helmet    carved head    oar    wooden shield    sword

## ▼ Life in a castle

*In the Middle Ages, kings and queens lived in big castles with thick walls. They were often attacked by their enemies.*

defense tower

tower

battlements

gatehouse

portcullis

## ▲ Arab scholars

*The Arabs were great scholars. They studied the stars, geography, and math.*

## ▲ Japanese samurai

*Japan also had castles and armored knights. These knights were called samurai. They fought with bows, arrows, and deadly sharp swords.*

## word search

**Christian** a person who believes in the teachings of Jesus Christ.
**Muslim** a person who follows the Prophet Muhammad's teaching.

# The age of discovery

In the late 1400s, a new age of learning began in northern Italy. People studied the books of ancient Greece and Rome. They wrote poetry and painted wonderful pictures. Europeans thought up many clever new inventions, such as printing presses, pocket watches, thermometers, and telescopes. At the same time, sailors from Portugal and Spain were traveling to distant lands in Africa, Asia, and the Americas. They were looking for precious spices and gold, and for new lands to conquer. Some European explorers even killed the local people or forced them to become slaves.

▲ **Columbus reaches the Caribbean**

*Christopher Columbus was an Italian explorer who worked for the Spanish king and queen. He sailed across the Atlantic Ocean in 1492, reaching the islands of the Caribbean Sea.*

10,000   9000   8000   7000   6000   5000   4000   3000   2000   1000   BC   0   AD   1000   2000

### ▼ Leonardo da Vinci

*Leonardo da Vinci lived in Italy in the 15th century. He was a great painter and sculptor. He was also an architect, an engineer, a scientist, and an inventor.*

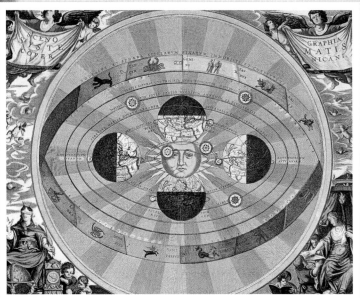

### ▲ Elizabeth 1 of England

*Elizabeth's reign is often called the Golden Age because it was a time of discovery and wealth for England in the 16th century.*

### ▲ Martin Luther

*Martin Luther was a Christian monk from Germany. In 1517, he protested against the Catholic Church, which was in Rome. His supporters were called Protestants.*

## word search

**explorer** a person who travels to find new things.

**invention** a new thing that has been made.

### ▲ Copernicus

*Copernicus, a Polish astronomer, published a book in 1543 that claimed the Earth moved around the Sun. Until then, most people believed that the Sun circled around the Earth.*

# The factory age

**During the 1700s, northern Europeans invented many new machines that were powered by water or by steam.** They built canals across the countryside and used barges to carry goods such as cloth and pottery from new factories. By the middle of the 19th century, steam trains were puffing through the fields of Europe and North America. There were new cotton mills and coal mines. More and more people left their villages to look for work in the new cities. While most workers were very poor in the 1800s, the owners of some factories grew very rich.

▼ **The first passenger railroad**

*The first steam-powered railroad to carry passengers ran from Stockton to Darlington, in England. It opened in 1825.*

## word search

**barge** a long boat with a flat bottom.
**canal** a narrow stretch of water for boats and barges to travel along.

### ▶ Around the world

*Europeans took over more and more land around the world in the 1700s and 1800s. This picture shows the Indians fighting the British in the Indian Mutiny. It developed into a battle against the British ruling India.*

### ◀ Industrial Britain

*The age of factories started in Britain and soon spread to northern Europe and America. Smoke from factory chimneys blackened towns and cities and even the surrounding countryside.*

### ▶ The French Revolution

*During the French Revolution, which began in 1789, King Louis XVI and many French lords and ladies were executed in front of large crowds. They had their heads cut off by a sharp blade called the guillotine.*

10,000  9000  8000  7000  6000  5000  4000  3000  2000  1000  BC  0  AD  1000  2000

# The last 100 years

**The world seemed to become smaller in the 1900s.** Travel by motor vehicle and aircraft made it possible to move around more quickly and easily. By 1961 a Russian had become the first person to travel in space. The wonderful new inventions of the age could be heard about on radio, or seen at the movie theater, then on television and, today, on the internet. Everyday life was better in many ways. New medicines were developed, and most children could go to school. However, this was also a period of terrible warfare and cruelty, with two major world wars.

▼ **Motor cars**
*The Model T Ford was first introduced in 1908. It was an inexpensive car that more families could afford to buy.*

▲ **The world's first flight**
*The first successful plane flight took place on a beach in North Carolina in 1903. Orville Wright stayed airborne in* Flyer 1 *for a total of 12 seconds.*

### ◀ First World War

*Troops from many countries battled for their lives during the First World War (1914 to 1918).*

### ▼ Pop music

*The Beatles were a British band who topped popular music charts all over the world in the 1960s.*

### ▲ Great Depression

*In the late 1920s and 1930s, many people had no work. They waited in line for food to be handed out.*

### ◀ Astronauts in space

*Astronauts first walked in space in 1965. Just four years later, men landed on the Moon's surface for the very first time. They could now look down on their home planet.*

### ▲ Fighting disease

*Doctors became more successful in fighting dangerous diseases such as smallpox and tetanus. These diseases had previously killed thousands of people.*

# Life around the world today

**word search**

**population** the number of people living in a place.
**remote** distant, faraway.
**state** area of land that forms part of a country.

**Around 10,000 years ago, you could walk all day and see no one.** There were just six million people in the whole world. Today, about the same number of people live in the state of Tennessee or in Denmark. There are over six billion people in the world, and in 50 years' time, the world's population may be twice that. New medicines and better food supplies mean that many more people stay alive longer. Most people live in places where there is fresh water, land to farm, or fish to catch. Cities have grown up along trading or traveling routes.

▲ **How we look**
*People around the world are all much the same, although they sometimes look different. Some have dark skin, and some have light skin, while their hair may be black, brown, blond, or red. People of all types live throughout the world.*

There are only about 560 people living in the Vatican City.

◀ **People need water**

*These women in Africa are taking water from their village well. Humans need water to stay alive, to grow crops, and to raise their animals.*

▶ **Faraway places**

*Why do few people live on remote islands? The islands may be too small or have poor soil. They may have no fresh water. They may be too far away for people to trade easily.*

# Snacks from around the world

**All around the world, children eat snacks.** Look around your local supermarket for ingredients to make yourself an international snack.

**1** In Japan, sushi is a favorite. Fish is wrapped in rice and dried seaweed. Dip into soy sauce for a salty taste.

**2** Mexicans eat tortillas, which are pancakes. They fill them with spicy beans, salad, melted cheese, and sour cream to become tacos.

**3** Greek children fill pita bread with hummus (made from chickpeas and tahini), salad, and natural yogurt.

# Living in deserts

Deserts may be sandy or rocky, hot or cold, high or low, windy or sheltered – but they are all dry! Very few crops can grow in such dry conditions. The wind blows the sand and piles it up into huge heaps, which are called dunes. Some deserts are scorching hot and some are bitterly cold. A few people have learned how to survive in deserts. They may live by trading, carrying their goods across the desert by camel or truck. They stop at a place called an oasis, where they can find water. People who herd goats or camels move from one oasis to another, looking for water and fresh grass.

▲ **People of the Sahara desert**
*The Tuareg people live in the Sahara, in North Africa. It is the world's biggest desert. They wear long robes and cover their faces with cloth to keep out the sun and sand.*

## ▼ Finding water

*The San people live in and around the Kalahari desert, in southern Africa. They sometimes use a reed to suck water from a tree trunk.*

## word search

**nomad** someone who does not settle in one place, but travels from one place to another.

**oasis** a green place in the desert where there is a supply of water.

## ▼ Desert homes

*Some people live in towns on the edge of the desert. Others, who are always on the move, live in tents. These people are called nomads.*

desert houses, Yemen

## explain

Many desert animals hide underground during the day and only come out at night. Can you explain why?

## How do camels survive in the desert?

All camels have thick eyelashes and nostrils shaped to keep out the dust. They have wide padded feet for walking over sand. One-humped camels live in Africa, western Asia, and Australia. Two-humped camels live in central and eastern Asia. Fat stored in these humps allows them to travel for long periods without water or food.

Bedouin tent, Saudi Arabia

# Lands of ice and snow

The most northerly place in the world is the North Pole. It lies in the middle of the Arctic Ocean, much of which stays frozen solid all year-round. The lands around the ocean are bitterly cold. There are icy mountains and deep-frozen plains, called the tundra. The frozen land around the South Pole is called Antarctica. Nobody lives there, but some scientists work there in special bases. They mainly study the weather. Antarctica is the coldest and windiest place on Earth. Penguins live on the icy coast of Antarctica, and whales swim in the surrounding seas.

◀ **Northern and southern lights**
*Flickering lights sometimes glow in the night sky near the North Pole and South Pole.*

can you find?

*seal* *ice house* *polar bear* *kayak* *husky*

◀ **Amundsen**

*This man was first to reach the South Pole. Read about how he did this in the story below.*

**word search**

**kayak** a type of light canoe, covered with sealskin or canvas.
**reindeer** a deer found in Europe, Asia, and North America. It is sometimes called the caribou.
**tundra** deep-frozen plains where no trees can grow.

◀ **Reindeer herders**

*The Sami people live in the far north of Scandinavia. They keep reindeer for milk, meat, fur, and skins.*

# The race to the South Pole

Roald Amundsen lived in Norway. In 1909, he decided to try to become the first man to reach the South Pole. Robert Falcon Scott in Britain was already planning his second attempt, and so a race began.

On October 19, 1911, Amundsen and four companions set off with four light sleds, each pulled by 13 dogs. Despite the dangers, everything went well. Their excitement grew as they approached their goal. Had they been fast enough? Amundsen and his men were the first people to reach the South Pole, arriving there on December 14, 1911.

Five weeks later, Scott reached the South Pole, only to discover that Amundsen had been there first.

A true story

**37**

**When did Amundsen reach the South Pole? Who was racing Amundsen?**

# Life in the grasslands

**Grasses grow mainly where there is not enough rain for trees, but too much for a desert.** Grasslands are covered in tall, waving grasses or short, tough grasses, and they have different names around the world. In North America they are called prairies, and in Europe and Asia they are called steppes. Grasslands often have very rich soil that is good for growing crops. In many places, farmers have plowed the grasslands and planted different grass crops, such as wheat and barley. Grasses grown for food are called grains. Grasslands are also used for cattle ranching.

▲ **On the Masai steppe**
*The Masai steppe is an area of East African grassland dotted with trees. The Masai live here in villages, grazing their herds of cattle.*

### ▲ Cowboys

Cowboys enter contests to show their skill at riding and catching cattle and horses. These contests are called rodeos. This rodeo, called the Calgary Stampede, is in Canada.

### ▼ Mongolian grasslands

Mongolian children riding on grasslands at a local festival.

### ▲ Prairie hunters

Two hundred years ago, huge herds of bison lived on the prairies of Canada and the United States. They ate the grass and were hunted by the Native American people who lived there.

# In forests and woods

Conifer forests are found mostly in the cold, northern parts of the world, between the tundra and the grasslands. The tough needles of the fir trees survive even the harshest winters. In parts of the world where the climate is milder, there are woodlands where the trees lose their leaves each winter. Some tropical regions of the world are warm and damp, with heavy rainfall. The thick rain forests that grow here stay green and lush all year-round. All sorts of birds, insects, and snakes live in these forests.

**draw**

Draw a picture of a rain forest. Make sure you include the correct plants, trees, and animals that live there.

▲ **In the South American rain forest**
*The Yanomami are among people who live in in the rain forests of South America. They hunt, fish, and grow food in the forest.*

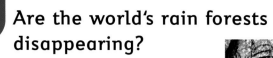

## Are the world's rain forests disappearing?

Over hundreds of years, a lot of forests and woodlands have been cut down to build homes or to burn as fuel. Farmers cleared the forests to make new fields. Today, people are aware of the danger of rain forests being destroyed. Plans are being made to take care of the world's rain forests.

▼ **The moose and the elk**
*This big deer lives in northern forests. It is called a moose in North America and an elk in Europe and Asia.*

▲ **Poison-arrow frog**
*Poison taken from this frog is smeared onto arrows by South American hunters. It helps to kill the animals they shoot.*

## word search

**conifers** trees that produce cones. Most are evergreen trees.
**needle** pointed leaf of a pine or fir tree.
**rain forest** area of dense, green forest that is found in the hot and rainy lands of South America, Africa, southern Asia, and northeast Australia.

▲ **The Mbuti people**
*The Mbuti, a group of pygmies, hunt wild animals and gather roots and fruits to eat. Some of the African rain forest where they live is being destroyed.*

# Mountains and valleys

Mountains are difficult and sometimes dangerous places in which to live. The upper slopes are cold and windy, and may be covered in snow. It is hard to build roads or railroads through mountains. The weather may be too harsh for farming, although in some mountain areas people manage to raise cows, goats, and sheep, or to grow crops in sheltered valleys. Forests on mountain slopes may be cut for timber. The water from mountain streams and lakes is useful too. It may provide drinking water or be used to power machines that make electricity.

◀ **Farming in Switzerland**
*Each spring, as the snow melts, Swiss cattle are led up the mountain to high pastures. In the fall they are led down again to spend the cold winter in the sheltered valley.*

▲ **Houses in the Andes**
*Houses can be found high on the mountain slopes of the Andes in South America.*

## word search

**lava** liquid rock that bursts from inside the Earth.
**pasture** grass used for grazing cattle or sheep.
**terrace** a step cut into the side of a mountain.

#### ▼ Himalayan farming

*The Nepalese people have learned how to grow crops on steep slopes. Steps called terraces prevent soil from being washed away.*

#### ▲ Volcano danger

*Some mountains are volcanoes. The people who settle on the slopes are in danger from eruptions of lava and ash. However, the soil around volcanoes is often very rich.*

# To move mountains

There was once an old man named Yugong who lived near two high mountains in China. Every time anyone from his village wanted to go anywhere, they had to take a very long route around the mountains. "If we could flatten these mountains we could reach the south and the Han River easily," Yugong said. Everyone agreed but could not see how to flatten them.

Yugong had made up his mind. He took his three sons and grandsons and together they worked all winter and summer breaking rocks, and carrying the rubble away to the Bo Sea.

The king of the gods admired Yugong's determination, and asked two strong gods to move the rest of the mountains for them. From that day on, no mountain blocked the way to the south and the Han River.

Chinese fable

**What do you learn from this fable?  Which river was blocked by the mountains?**  **43**

# Living by water

**find out**

Why can't people drink the water in the oceans?

**More than two-thirds of our planet is covered in water.** Rain brings water to the land and keeps plants, animals, and people alive. The rain runs into rivers and lakes, and provides fresh water for drinking. The rivers run into the oceans. Here, the water is too salty to drink. People live near water so that they can fish, and build and use boats. Seaports are busy centers for shipping and trade. Sea walls and dams are built to prevent the sea water from flooding over low-lying land. Sometimes the sea can be pushed back to make areas of dry land.

▲ **Portuguese fishermen**
*Portuguese fishermen mend their nets when they are not at sea catching fish.*

▲ **On Lake Titicaca**
*On this South American lake, reeds are used to make island houses and boats.*

## word search

**canal** a river or waterway built by people.
**dam** a big barrier, built of soil, stone, or concrete, that stops the flow of water.
**sampan** a small covered boat in China. The word means "three boards."

### ▶ A home on water

*Many people make their homes in these small boats, called sampans, in the harbors of Hong Kong, China.*

### ▲ Canals in Venice

*The city of Venice, in Italy, is surrounded by the ocean. It has many canals, which take the place of streets.*

### ▲ Houses on stilts

*Houses are often raised on long poles to prevent them from being washed away in a flood. These stilt houses are in Papua New Guinea.*

# Life in the country

## About half of the world's population lives in the countryside.

In the country there are no big cities, only small towns and villages. Most of the land is taken up by farms and fields, or by large areas of forests, mountains, or lakes. The countryside is often cleaner and quieter than the city. In some parts of the world, country people may live long distances from the nearest town. There are few roads and schools, and sometimes there are few jobs. Many young people leave to look for work in the cities.

▲ **Keeping in touch**
*Children living on remote farms in Australia are often far away from the nearest school. Some use the radio or the internet to keep in touch with their teachers.*

▲ **Village work**
*In some country villages, all the people are expected to help when crops are harvested. These villagers are working in rice fields on an island called Bali, in Indonesia.*

**word search**

**remote** far away, distant.
**thatch** to cover a roof with reeds or straw.

**Yellowstone Park**

**Kenyan National Park**

## ▲ National parks

*Sometimes areas of the countryside are set aside as national parks. Yellowstone, created in 1872 in America, is the world's oldest national park.*

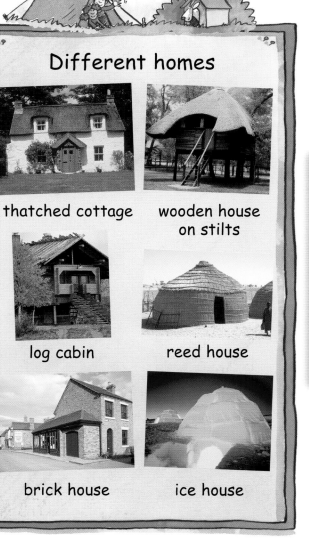

## Different homes

thatched cottage

wooden house on stilts

log cabin

reed house

brick house

ice house

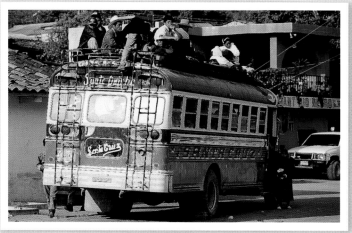

## ▲ Travel in the country

*In South America, crowded buses carry people and their goods over bumpy country roads. Many remote villages have no electricity and no piped water.*

In New Zealand there are 10 times as many sheep as people.

# The town mouse and the country mouse

A little mouse lived next to a cornfield in the country. She had a small, cozy cottage where she felt comfortable and safe. There was nothing to disturb her peaceful life. One day her cousin from the town came to visit. The town mouse climbed down from her carriage. She straightened her fancy hat and picked up her suitcase. The two little mice rubbed whiskers and said hello.

1 "What a beautiful place for a vacation," said the town mouse. "Lovely, fresh country air," she said as she sniffed the lavender growing next to her cousin's cottage.

2 Just then a tractor rumbled past and the town mouse dove for cover beneath the hedge. When a cow mooed loudly in her ear, she shook with terror.

3 "She won't hurt," said the country mouse, leading her cousin into her home. They sat down for supper – grains, nuts, and berries. The country mouse's favorite.

4 The town mouse did not think much of this plain food. "You should see what I eat at home," she said. "Come and stay with me."

What do you think might scare the town mouse in the country?

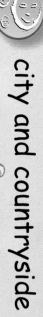

5 The two mice took the first cart back to town. When they arrived, the country mouse was afraid of being crushed. She had never seen anywhere so busy.

6 They scampered into the town mouse's home, straight to the kitchen. There were lots of delicious-looking foods to eat but the country mouse could not stop looking at the large cat asleep near the fire.

7 "Relax. Try some of this cheese," said the town mouse. Just then the cook walked in and screamed at the sight of the two mice. This woke the cat. The little mice scooted into a mousehole, narrowly escaping a sharp set of claws.

8 It was all too much for the country mouse. Her cousin was happy in the town, but she could not wait to go back to her small, cozy country cottage.

Aesop fable

What do you think might scare the country mouse in the town?

# City life

**Cities are busy, noisy, and crowded.**
In the center are offices, stores, hotels, restaurants, theaters, and museums. Many people come into the city center during the day to work. The streets are busy with honking cars and taxis and crowded buses. Many more people live in the suburbs, on the edges of the city. Underneath the city sidewalks, there are pipes carrying gas and water to the buildings. Big sewers and drains carry away wastewater and rain. There are thousands of miles of electricity, telephone, and television cables. There are also underground road and rail tunnels.

▲ **Underground travel**
*Subways take people quickly from one side of the city to the other. This is the Metro (subway) in Paris, France.*

▼ **Dirty air**
*Traffic jams in large cities often make the air dirty and bad for us to breathe.*

## word search

**cables** bundles of wires.
**sewer** large drains that carry waste away from buildings.
**suburbs** the edges of a big town or city.

▲ **City bikes**
*The streets of most Chinese cities are filled with bicycles. They are cleaner and healthier to use than cars.*

The world's first underground railroad opened in London, UK, in 1863.

◀ **Skyscraper city**

*Seattle is the largest city in the U.S. state of Washington. Like many American cities, Seattle has giant skyscrapers framing its skyline. The Space Needle building (center) is an observation tower that gives fantastic views over the city.*

▼ **Poor people in the city**

*Many poor people have come to the Brazilian city of São Paulo to look for work. They live in shacks made of wood and tin.*

 **What is a skyscraper?**

The first skyscrapers were built in the United States over 120 years ago. They were built around strong steel frames. Electric elevators had just been invented, so people no longer had to climb stairs to the upper floors. This skyscraper is in Singapore.

# Let's talk

**This book is written in the English language.** About 6,000 different languages may be spoken in the world today. Over one billion people speak the Chinese language. English, French, and Spanish can be heard in many different parts of the world, too. Over 5,000 years ago, people learned how to write down languages. They used all sorts of marks and little pictures. Each one stood for a sound or an idea. Many kinds of alphabets and symbols are used today. They are called scripts.

▲ **Picture writing**
*These symbols are called hieroglyphs. They were first used for writing in ancient Egypt 5,200 years ago (see page 17).*

▲ **Written by monks**
*About 800 years ago in Europe, monks copied out beautiful books by hand, using ink and pens made from goose feathers. These books are called illuminated manuscripts.*

thank you
ありがとう
ευχαριστώ
شكراً
спасибо
gracias

▲ **Different alphabets**
*Not all alphabets are the same. Here are six different ways of writing "thank you." They are (from top to bottom) English, Japanese, Greek, Arabic, Russian, and Spanish.*

## word search

**alphabet** a collection of letters used to make words.

**interpreter** someone who translates what you say into another language.

**script** a way of writing out speech by the use of letters or symbols.

### ▼ Communicating without words

*We can use our hands as well as words to put across our thoughts and ideas. What do you think these hands are saying?*

### ▼ Chinese writing

*It is possible to use over 80,000 different symbols or marks when you write in Chinese. Children don't have to learn all of them, and most people use only about 5,000. The symbols are called characters.*

### ▶ First words

*Babies start off by crying and making noises in order to tell us what they want. Later they learn to speak words.*

### Good day!

French Bonjour!
German Guten Tag!
Spanish ¡Buenos días!
Italian Buon giorno!
Swahili Shikamoo!
Chinese Ni hao!

### ▲ Hundreds of languages

*Over 800 languages are spoken in Papua New Guinea. In many areas of the country, people need to use an interpreter to talk to each other.*

Human speech includes about 44 basic sounds called phonemes.

# What do you wear?

**We wear clothes to protect our bodies from the weather and to look good.** Most people in the world wear suits, dresses, jeans, shorts, or T-shirts. Some clothing is suitable for particular places. For instance, in the Sahara desert people wear loose robes to stay cool. In the Arctic, people wear thick coats to keep warm. In India, women often wear cotton or silk dresses called saris. In some lands, people wear shells and feathers and paint their faces and bodies.

▼ **Clothes around the world**

*People wear different types of clothing. Do you know why these people are all dressed differently?*

Kamayurà man from Brazil

Arab woman

Japanese girl

Indian woman

Inuit man from Greenland

Herera woman from Namibia

The ancient Egyptians were using makeup about 5,000 years ago.

**▲ On the catwalk**

Cats don't go on a catwalk, but fashion models do! It's a long stage where models can show off the latest clothing designs.

**▼ Religious clothing**

This man is a Buddhist monk. He wears an orange robe to show his faith.

**▲ Wearing uniforms**

In an emergency, we need to recognize police officers. This is why they wear uniforms, making them stand out from other people.

# Zeus and the jackdaw

**Z**eus, the most important god in Ancient Greece, **decided the birds should have a king.** He told them he would choose the most handsome bird to be their leader. The birds flew away to the river where they chattered and washed, preening their feathers to make them gleam. The jackdaw wanted to be king but he knew he would never be chosen because his feathers were too dull. When the others left, he quickly picked up the feathers they had dropped and attached them to his own. He joined the others at the palace, looking very colorful in his borrowed plumes. "You are the finest," said Zeus. "You will be king."

The jackdaw strutted toward the throne and a feather fell off. Then another and another. Everyone could see who he really was. The jackdaw hid his head, and Zeus chose another bird to be king.

Aesop fable

What do you think the jackdaw learned?  Who was Zeus?

55

# Money and markets

Before people had money, they used to swap or trade the things they needed. At the market, a farmer might swap his cow for three sacks of flour. Later, people began to use tokens of value, such as shells or beads. The most useful tokens were metal coins. Today we use coins, paper bills, and plastic cards to buy things. Most countries in the world have their own coins and paper money. They are called currencies. For example, the US currency is the dollar, which is made up of 100 cents. People are paid with money for the work they do.

▲ **In the bank**
*All over the world, banks exchange different currencies. They charge customers extra for borrowing money and give money to those who save. These fees and payments are called interest.*

## draw

Paper money has very complicated designs so that it is hard to copy. Can you design some new money?

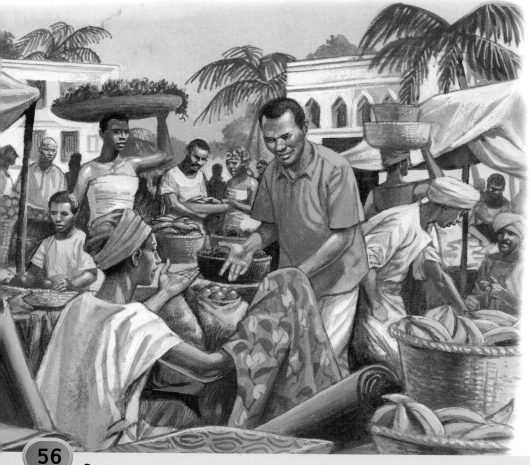

◀ **In the market**
*This open-air market is in Nigeria in Africa. Here you can buy all sorts of things — peanuts, dried fish, dark glasses, batteries, meat, bananas, hats, watches, and shirts. Everybody argues about the prices.*

Paper money was invented in China about 1,200 years ago.

### ▶ Ancient traders

*The ancient Sumerians used clay tokens instead of money. This trader is paying for an animal.*

clay token

### word search

**currency** the type of money normally used in a country.
**interest** extra money paid by the bank to savers, or to the bank by borrowers.
**manufactured** something made by hand/with machines.

### ▲ Making money
*Millions of coins are manufactured in a special factory called a mint.*

---

# Trading beads

## Traders who visited Africa long ago used glass beads as money.
Make your own trading beads to wear as a bracelet or necklace.

### You will need
- self-hardening clay in different colors · rolling pin
- thin knitting needle · knife · varnish · thread or elastic

**1** Roll out long pieces of colored clay and lay them together. Cover these with another layer of clay. Roll this out, then cut out bead shapes.

**2** Push a knitting needle through each bead to make a hole. When the beads have hardened, give them a coat of varnish and thread them to make a bracelet or necklace.

**Read more about other things people have used as money on page 56.**

# Buying and selling

▲ **Supermarket**

*In supermarkets, all sorts of goods can be bought in the same place. It makes life easier for the shopper, but smaller stores find it hard to compete with such big stores.*

All over the world, people live by buying and selling all kinds of goods, from toys and clothes to furniture and cars. People who supply goods to the stores are called wholesalers. People who supply goods to the public, from stores, supermarkets, convenience stores, or markets, are called retailers. Most offices are in town and city centers. Office workers may organize the way in which goods are made, transported, or sold, or they may provide other services, such as banking or insurance.

▼ **Outdoor market**

*People come to this outdoor market in Portugal to buy and sell fresh fruit and vegetables.*

### ▼ Architects at work

*Many architects design buildings, from houses to churches. These designs are bought by the customers who want to make the buildings.*

## word search

**law** a set of rules that people must follow.
**retail** when goods are sold to the public.
**services** useful jobs that people pay others to do.
**wholesale** when goods are sold in large amounts to stores before they are sold to the public.

### ▼ Working as a lawyer

*A lawyer is trained in all aspects of the law. People pay a lawyer for his help and advice on legal matters, such as buying a house.*

### ◄ Ice cream vendor

*Lots of businesses sell their goods on busy streets. An ice cream cart moves from one place to another, in order to sell the most ice cream.*

**The world's biggest shopping center is in Edmonton, Canada.**

# Working on the land

The land provides different kinds of work for many people. Farmers grow all sorts of food crops, such as wheat, rice, fruit, or vegetables. They plow the soil and plant seeds, sometimes using tractors. They harvest the crops. Other farmers raise cattle, sheep, or chickens. Foresters plant trees and cut them for timber. Miners tunnel underground to get coal or metals such as tin or gold. Engineers dam rivers and build big bridges and roads. First, they blast out rock and use bulldozers, steam shovels, and rollers to clear the land.

▲ **Forestry work**

*Lumberjacks use big saws. Forests in Finland provide timber for building and for making furniture, paper, and matches.*

▼ **Tea picking**

*These women in India are picking fresh leaves from tea bushes. The dried tea leaves are sold all over the world.*

▲ **Sheep farming**

*In New Zealand, millions of sheep are raised for their meat and wool.*

## word search

**bulldozer** a huge machine used for moving soil.
**harvest** to gather in crops.
**lumberjack** someone who cuts down trees.
**plow** to turn over soil.

### ▶ On the farm

*Pigs, geese, and chickens are just a few of the animals that are raised by this European farmer. The farmer sells his produce to local businesses.*

### Do all farmers sell the food they grow?

Many small farms may produce just enough food for the farmer's own family. Any extra can be sold at the local market. However, some farms are very big. They produce large amounts of crops that can be sold in the cities or overseas.

### ▼ Drilling for gold

*This South African miner is drilling for gold deep under the ground.*

## remember

What do you call someone whose job it is to cut down trees?

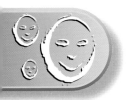

# Working at sea

Some people spend much of their lives working at sea. Some are sailors on big oil tankers, on passenger ferries, or on container ships. Others sail on trawlers, hauling in nets full of fish. On many trawlers, the fish are cut up and frozen while the boat is still at sea. Engineers drill down to get oil and gas from under the ocean floor. Many oil rigs and platforms are out at sea. The workers travel to and from the rigs by helicopter or boat.

▼ **Exploring the ocean**

*This mini-submarine takes scientists down to explore the depths of the ocean.*

ALVIN

**Fishing at sea**

*High waves are breaking over this fishing boat. The crew wear waterproof clothes while they haul in the nets.*

## word search

**container ship** a ship that transports goods in large metal boxes.

**submarine** a ship that travels under the water.

**trawler** a boat that pulls long fishing nets.

# The fisherman and the talking fish

**A** poor fisherman lived with his wife in a hut near the ocean. One day when he was hard at work he caught a large fish. "Spare me, let me live," gasped the fish, to the fisherman's surprise. "I am an enchanted prince. Please put me back into the water."

The fisherman agreed at once and later told his wife all about the talking fish.

"Why didn't you ask him for anything?" said his wife, Alice. "We live in this awful little hut. Go back and ask for a cottage."

The fisherman did not like this very much, but he went back to the water's edge and called. The fish soon swam by and when he heard what the fisherman's wife wanted he said, "Go home, she's in the cottage already."

Sure enough, the fisherman found Alice in a pretty cottage. She was happy – for only a week.

"This cottage is too small. I want a castle," she complained. "Ask the fish."

Reluctantly the fisherman asked. When he got home, Alice stood at the door of a grand castle. Next morning, Alice shook him awake. "I must be Queen," she said. "Go to the fish."

The castle became a palace and Alice sat on a golden throne, a jeweled crown on her head. Still she was not satisfied. Twice more she sent her husband to the talking fish, first to be made emperor and then pope. The fish granted her wishes, but Alice could not sleep at night because of wondering what she could be next. As the Sun rose, she had an idea.

"I must be lord of the Sun and Moon," she said. "Go to the fish at once."

The fisherman was very afraid but there was no point arguing. As he reached the ocean a wind began to blow. The sky grew black and waves crashed onto the shore. "What now?" asked the fish.

"She wants to be lord of the Sun and Moon," whispered the fisherman.

"Go home to your hut," said the fish. And there the fisherman and his wife stayed. The fish would not grant any more wishes.

Traditional fairytale

What was special about the fish? What do you learn from the story?

# Making things

**Some people work by making or repairing things.** They may be craft workers, making pottery by hand or weaving fine cloth. They may be tailors who stitch and sew cloth. They may be construction workers laying bricks, carpenters sawing wood, or shipyard workers putting an anchor onto a big ship. In factories, goods such as cars, televisions, cakes, or bottles can be made quickly, in large numbers. Cars are put together piece by piece, on assembly lines. Some of the work, such as paint spraying, is done by robots.

▼ **Carpet craft**

*This woman from Turkmenistan is making a fine-quality, richly colored carpet.*

◄ **Handwoven hats**

*Many women in Ecuador make a living by making straw hats. This woman is weaving the straw by hand.*

► **Painting bark**

*This aboriginal artist from Australia is painting a fish on bark. The ideas for the paintings often come from ancient myths.*

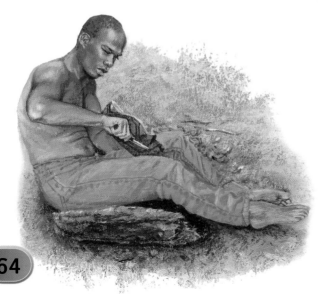

◄ **Carving wood**

*Many African people, such as the Makonde of Tanzania, are expert at carving hardwoods.*

## word search

**kiln** a very hot oven used to bake clay objects.

▼ **Working with your hands**

*A potter shapes the wet clay by hand as it whirls around on a wheel. When the bowl is ready, it will be baked hard in a kiln.*

▲ **Classroom crafts**

*You too can make things. These schoolgirls from the Caribbean island of Saint Lucia are printmaking.*

▼ **Car factory**

*Cars are made in big factories. As they pass down the assembly line, they are put together by robots as well as by people.*

## make

Make one of the different projects in this book. Look at the photos below to help you decide.

**Things to make in this book**

village from long ago

trading beads

Mexican tacos

magnetic game

Over 15 million Model T Ford cars were sold between 1908 and 1927.

# Helping others

**Many jobs are about helping other people.** Doctors and nurses help sick and injured people get better. Teachers help children learn. The police catch criminals. Firefighters risk their lives to save others. Volunteers help other people by joining lifeboat crews or mountain rescue teams. Many young people help others too. Some learn to give first aid, and others help elderly people or take care of children.

▶ **To the rescue**

*A lifeboat steers through huge waves to rescue people from a sinking ship.*

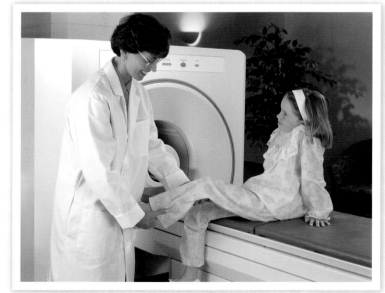

▲ **A helping hand**

*Doctors work in medical centers, clinics, and hospitals. This one is helping a young girl get better, after she has injured her leg.*

## Helping out

wash the dog

read a story

weed the garden

go for a walk

▲ **Firefighters**

*Firefighters put out the flames by squirting water through powerful hoses. The fire engine has long ladders so that the firefighters can rescue people from tall buildings.*

## word search

**first aid** the correct way to treat sick or injured people before a doctor or ambulance arrives.

**lifeboat** a boat that goes to rescue people in trouble at sea.

**volunteer** somebody who offers to help, for no payment or other reward.

▶ **Teacher and student**

*Teachers help children learn different skills at school. As well as reading and writing, children can learn about different languages, history, geography, and art.*

## Who rescues people in the mountains?

If someone has an accident in the mountains, a team of rescue workers may have to go look for the injured person. They often use specially trained dogs to find people buried under the snow. Then they carry them down the mountain on stretchers. Sometimes injured people are rescued by helicopter.

67

# In holy places

Over the ages, many different religious faiths have grown up around the world. Some people believe in one God; others believe in many different gods and spirits.

**▲ Jesus Christ**
*This scene shows Jesus Christ. He was born about 2,000 years ago. Christians believe he was the son of God.*

**▶ Pilgrims to Mecca**
*Muslims believe that there is one God, whose messenger was the Prophet Muhammad, who lived 1,400 years ago. Each year, about two million Muslim pilgrims visit Mecca.*

**▲ A Jewish rabbi**
*The holy teachings of the Jews are written down in the Torah. This rabbi is reading from a copy of it.*

**▲ The 5 Ks**
*Most religions have their own special customs. Sikh men and boys always wear the "5 Ks."*
1. *kanga — comb symbolizing personal hygiene*
2. *kirpan — sword symbolizing resistance against evil*
3. *kara — metal bracelet symbolizing faithfulness to God*
4. *kacch — white cotton, knee-length underpants symbolizing purity*
5. *kesh — uncut hair covered by a turban*

**word search**

**monk** religious person who lives in a monastery.
**pilgrim** someone who makes a journey in honor of a god or gods.
**rabbi** Jewish religious leader.

◄ **Buddhist monks**

*These monks in Tibet follow the teachings of Siddhartha Gautama, known as the Buddha, who lived in India about 2,550 years ago. He gave up all his wealth to live the simple life of a monk.*

▶ **Beside the Ganges**

*For Hindus, the Ganges is a holy river. They bathe in its water at the Indian city of Varanasi.*

# Christmas story boxes

**Make your own story boxes to hang on the Christmas tree.**

These biblical scenes were taken to South America to teach people the Bible.

**1** Take the small box and cut off the top. Make doors to fit from the top of the box or from two pieces of construction paper. Attach them to the box with tape. Paint the box and decorate with glitter.

## You will need

small box · scissors · construction paper · glue and brush · tape · paint and paintbrushes · self-hardening clay in different colors · glitter

**2** Make clay models of Joseph, Mary, Baby Jesus, the shepherds, sheep, and the Three Wise Men. Decorate your models with paint and glitter.

**3** Cut out a circle of construction paper and glue your nativity figures in place.

Read more about the different religions on these pages.

# Special days

**We enjoy festivals, holidays, and other special days.** Many festivals are religious. Christmas is the time when Christians celebrate the birth of Christ. The feast of Eid ul-Fitr marks the end of the Muslim month of Ramadan, when no food may be eaten during the daytime. Some festivals mark the passing of the seasons, such as New Year, springtime, or harvest. And some festivals are just for fun. Family celebrations are held to mark birthdays, Mother's Day, weddings, and anniversaries. They are celebrated with presents, cards, flowers, special clothes, and meals.

▲ **Chinese New Year**
*The Chinese New Year is celebrated in January or February each year. Dancers inside a long paper dragon weave through the streets. Firecrackers explode to scare away evil spirits.*

◄ **"Happy Birthday to You"**
*Your birthday is the day that you were born. You celebrate with your family and friends.*

In 1969, astronauts in space sang "Happy Birthday to You."

**◀ Carnivals**

*Carnivals started as religious festivals, but today they are held for fun. In this carnival in Rio de Janeiro, Brazil, people dance in the streets wearing colorful costumes.*

## ▲ A Hindu wedding

*A special feast takes place to mark a Hindu wedding. The bride and groom wear garlands of flowers and make their vows to each other.*

## Who is St. Nicholas?

St Nicholas, or Sinterklaas, was a bishop who lived 1,600 years ago. He was generous and became the model for Sinterklaas (Dutch for Santa Claus). He is said to arrive in Amsterdam, in the Netherlands, on December 5 — on a boat from Spain. Children leave out carrots and hay in clogs (wooden shoes) for his horse to eat.

## word search

**carnival** a festival first held by Christians in Europe before Lent, a long period of going without food. Carnivals today are marked by dancing, costumes, and feasting.

**celebrate** to do something fun on a special occasion, such as having a party.

**festival** a feast or special day (or days).

# Hobbies and games

**Collecting can be fun and is a good way of finding out all sorts of interesting information.** Shells, flowers, stamps, labels, dolls, and foreign coins make good collections. Many African children make hoops from bicycle wheels. Children in India and China are experts at making paper kites. Children everywhere play different kinds of running games, tag, hopscotch, and leapfrog. Card games and board games, such as chess or Chinese checkers, are enjoyed by grown-ups as well as children. During the 1980s, computer games became very popular. These games are now played by millions of children around the world.

**word search**

**hopscotch** a game of hopping and jumping over squares marked on the ground.
**tag** any running, chasing, and catching game.

ball games

hula-hoop

jumping rope

hopscotch

tag

▲ **Playground games**
*Games are fun and can be played almost anywhere. They keep us fit and healthy. Hopscotch helps with counting, too.*

◀ **Shells from the seaside**
*These children are collecting empty shells at the beach. You can stick them on a box and varnish it.*

▼ **Making things**
*Have you ever made things from everyday items? This African boy has made a bus.*

▲ **The oldest board game**
*The oldest known board game is 4,500 years old. It was played by princes and princesses in a city called Ur, in western Asia. The beautiful board and pieces have survived, but we don't know the rules.*

▼ **Kite flying**
*The Chinese were flying paper kites shaped like birds over 3,000 years ago.*

▼ **A stamp album**
*People collect stamps and put them in stamp albums. Pictures on the stamps help us to find out about other countries – their history, people, and wildlife.*

**find out**

How many playing cards are there in a deck? What are the four different suits?

# The world of sports

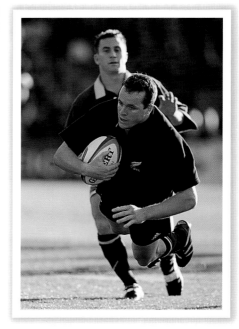

**Sports keep us fit and healthy.** They are exciting, too, whether we play or watch. Some sports, such as the high jump or sprinting, depend on the skill and strength of just one person. Others, such as basketball, need people to work together as a team. Some sports, such as sailing or skiing, depend on the skillful use of equipment. Many sports started out as simple children's games. Kicking a ball turned into all kinds of football games with different rules, field markings, and team numbers. At least six different types of football are played around the world today.

▲ **Rugby Union**
*Rugby Union is a type of football game played in many parts of the world. A 'try' is when you touch the ball down behind the other team's line.*

▼ **Outdoor activities**
*Cycling, waterskiing, and snowskiing are sports that are fun to watch, and even more fun to take part in. They are good ways of staying in shape.*

▲ **World's most popular sport**
*Soccer is the world's most popular sport.*

▲ **Teamwork**
*Sports teach us all kinds of skills. They help us to work together as a team, too. These athletes are playing basketball.*

## word search

**sprinting** running at high speed over a short distance.

▲ **Softball**
*Children play softball in a neighborhood park.*

The world's fastest ball game is called pelota, or jaï alaï.

# Olympic Games

The Olympic Games began in Olympia, ancient Greece, in 776 BC. This ancient sporting contest is still held every four years, taking place in a different city each time. Athletes come from all over the world to take part. Winter Olympic Games have also been held every four years since 1924. They are for sports such as skiing and ice-skating.

### ▼ The winners

*The top three athletes in each contest receive an Olympic medal – a gold for first, silver for second, and bronze for third. This athlete has won a gold for the 400-meter sprint.*

### ▲ Olympic stadium

*The track surrounds the field where events such as discus throwing take place.*

### ▶ Pool champion

*Swimming and water sports are major Olympic events. This American swimmer has just competed in the 200-meter breaststroke.*

### ▲ Track events

*Short, fast sprints and longer, slower races require different skills.*

# Rollerblade magnetic game

**Time how fast your rollerblader can race.** Get your friends to make their own players and, using the hidden magnet, race your rollerbladers around the course.

## You will need
- 14 x 18 in (36 x 45 cm) cardboard
- 1½ x 16 in (4 x 40 cm) cardboard
- 8 x 18 in (20 x 45 cm) black paper
- construction paper • colored felt
- red paper • two pieces of green felt, 3 x 18 in (8 x 45 cm) • felt markers
- magnets • glue and brush

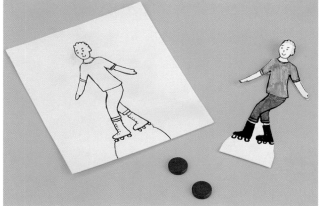

**1** Draw a picture of a rollerblader on the construction paper. Cut out your rollerblader and decorate it with felt-tip pens. Remember to leave a white strip at the base of the rollerblader. Fold back this white strip and stick on two magnets.

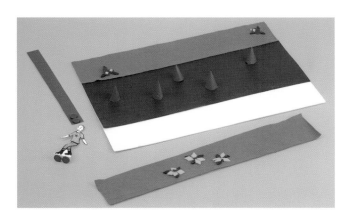

**2** Cover the larger sheet of cardboard with a thin layer of glue. Place the black paper across the center of the cardboard. Place the green felt strips along either side of the black strip. Decorate the grass with flowers made from colored felt. Roll up pieces of the red paper and glue the edges together to make the cones. Stick them on the track. Take the strip of cardboard and attach two more magnets to the end.

**3** Stand your rollerblader on the track. Place the strip of cardboard with magnets at the end under the cardboard and below the rollerblader. As you move the magnetic strip along, the rollerblader will skate along the track. Race your friends and see who can complete the course in the fastest time.

# Reading for fun

## What is the big news story today?

Newspapers tell us what is going on in the world. Books give us exciting stories and beautiful pictures. Comics and cartoon strips make us laugh. Magazines tell us all we need to know about our hobbies or interests. Making newspapers, magazines, and books is called publishing. An author types the words onto a computer. The writing is checked and corrected by an editor. A designer uses a computer to make up each page, arranging the words and pictures on the screen. The book is then ready to be printed.

Alice in Wonderland

Peter Pan

The Wind in the Willows

▲ **Famous characters**
*All these well-known characters appear in popular children's storybooks.*

**tell**

Retell the story of a book you have read recently. Do you know the author's name?

◄ **Storytelling**
*You can borrow books from your local library. Storytelling sessions may be held there, too.*

▶ **Illustrated books**

*Some books contain a lot of pictures. Artists who draw and paint these pictures are called illustrators.*

▼ **In a bookstore**

*Thousands of books are published every year. In a bookstore you will find books on everything from cats to cabbages.*

## word search

**author** the writer of a book, poem, or article in a newspaper or magazine.
**cartoon strip** a story told in pictures.
**publish** to get a book printed and sent out to the bookstores.

## What were the first children's stories?

These stories were tales told by grandparents and parents to their children. These tales began to be written down and published about 300 years ago. Soon writers began to make up their own stories for children. Comics and cartoon strips first became popular over 100 years ago. Can you tell which story this picture comes from?

In 1317, the Chinese published an encyclopedia with 348 chapters.

# The world of art

The first artists mixed their colors from natural substances such as black soot or red clay. Today, artists can buy paints in every color you can imagine. Some are made with water, others with oil or plastics. Artists can draw with chalks and pastels, pencils, crayons, and pens. Through the ages, artists have painted religious pictures, landscapes, and portraits. Some artists paint things they see in their dreams. Today's artists don't just work with paint. They may use light, sound, video, photographs, metal, plastic, everyday objects, or even living people.

▲ **The first artists**
*The first art was painted on cave walls by people who lived thousands of years ago.*

## word search

**canvas** a sheet of cotton or other fabric stretched over a frame for painting on.
**landscape** a painting of a view, such as country fields or city streets.
**portrait** a picture of a person's face.

◀ **Art galleries**
*Visit a gallery to see a selection of paintings. Notice how other people have painted and then try to paint a picture yourself.*

In Russia, the world's biggest art museum has nearly three million paintings.

**◄ Bright colors**

*Quick-drying acrylic paints are made from plastics. They come in brilliant colors.*

**► Watercolor paints**

*Watercolor paints are runny and quick-drying. They are often painted onto wet paper.*

**▲ Painting with oils**

*Oil paints come in strong colors. These paints are slow to dry. The artist can paint over the top once they have dried. They are painted onto board or canvas.*

# Window painting

**Decorate a window with a summer scene or picture of your choice.** Paint on the inside of windows because rain will wash off outdoor painting.

### You will need
- powder paints • water
- dishwashing detergent
- large paintbrushes
- newspaper

**1** Mix the paints with water and a few drops of detergent. Choose the window you are going to use and make sure you put newspaper down to catch the splashes.

**2** Start painting the glass, using your imagination to create wonderful window scenes.

Remember to ask an adult before starting to paint on any windows.

# Making music

Music is a combination of sounds that we make, to please ourselves or others. Music may be sung with our voices or made with musical instruments. Its beat, or timing, is called rhythm. The way in which one note follows another, to make a tune, is called melody. The way in which notes are combined at the same time is called harmony. People have played music for tens of thousands of years. The styles of music have varied greatly over the ages and from one part of the world to another.

▼ **Gamelan**

*This gentle, tinkling music is played in Indonesia. The children are learning how to strike the instruments.*

▲ **Steel band**

*The pans or steel drums are played in the Caribbean islands. They have a melodious sound.*

▲ **Flamenco**

*Some music is good for dancing to, like flamenco. This kind of dancing is very popular in Spain.*

## word search

**harmony** the arrangement of musical sounds so that they blend together pleasantly at the same time.
**melody** the arrangement of musical sounds, one after another, to form a tune.
**notes** a particular musical sound within a range of sounds, often shown by a written sign.
**rhythm** the timing or beat to which music is played.

### ▼ Folk songs
*These songs have often been handed down over the years. Joan Baez plays old and modern folk songs to the tune of a guitar.*

### ▼ Choirs
*A large number of people who sing together make up a choir. This choir is singing religious music in a Christian church.*

## listen

Listen to a CD or tape of an orchestra playing music. Which instruments do you think they are playing?

### ▲ Pop music
*Pop groups like the Backstreet Boys often play dance music with a strong beat.*

83

Bone whistles from over 25,000 years ago have been found in parts of Europe.

# Musical instruments

**Can you play music?** Some musical instruments make a sound when they are hit or shaken. They are called percussion instruments. Wind instruments need to be blown. Many instruments have strings. Guitar strings are often plucked with the fingers, but violins are played with a bow. All these instruments can be played together, either in a pop group or in a classical orchestra. Large orchestras need a conductor to make sure the players keep in time. Some modern instruments are made louder, or amplified, by electricity.

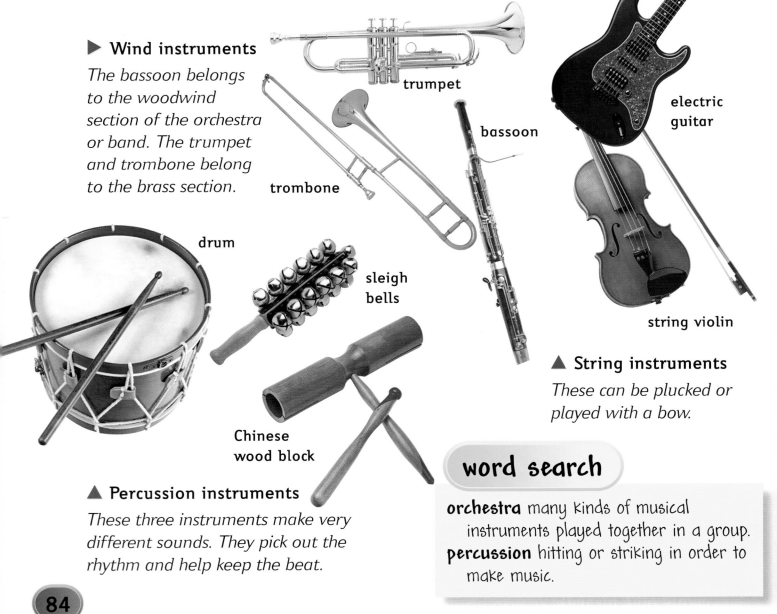

▶ **Wind instruments**
*The bassoon belongs to the woodwind section of the orchestra or band. The trumpet and trombone belong to the brass section.*

trumpet

bassoon

electric guitar

trombone

drum

sleigh bells

string violin

▲ **String instruments**
*These can be plucked or played with a bow.*

Chinese wood block

▲ **Percussion instruments**
*These three instruments make very different sounds. They pick out the rhythm and help keep the beat.*

## word search

**orchestra** many kinds of musical instruments played together in a group.
**percussion** hitting or striking in order to make music.

# Sir Orfeo's harp

**At the time of King Arthur, Sir Orfeo ruled a small kingdom.** His castle was a very merry one. Musicians were always welcome, and Orfeo liked to play the harp while his wife, Heurodis, sang.

One afternoon, Heurodis fell asleep beneath an apple tree. She woke suddenly and screamed. Then, to everyone's horror, she vanished. A snake slithered away, but there was no sign of Heurodis. Orfeo set out to find her, taking only his harp.

One day, he found a palace in a dense forest. A procession led by a king and queen was just about to go inside. Orfeo watched, his eyes drawn to one particular lady. When he saw her face, he knew why. It was Heurodis. He had to follow.

He found himself in a garden filled with people. Some were riding horses, many were asleep, and one even had a sword sticking into him. And then Orfeo saw Heurodis sleeping under an apple tree, a snake coiled around her wrist. With a shock, he realized everyone was dead and he was looking at how they died.

"Why are you here?" a voice asked harshly. Orfeo had not seen the king and queen on their thrones.

"I'm a visitor, here to play my harp," Orfeo said.

"This is the underworld," the king said. "People don't visit."

But the queen wanted Orfeo to play. And so he did. He played the most beautiful and saddest tune anyone had ever heard. He played for Heurodis and for his miserable years wandering lost and alone.

When he finished, the queen spoke. "As a reward for your wonderful music, you shall have anything you wish."

"Heurodis alive again," said Orfeo at once.

"No!" cried the king.

But the queen smiled, "Just this one time...."

After a long silence, the king agreed.

"Go quickly," said the queen. "And beware of snakes."

Arthurian legend

85

Why did Orfeo leave his castle? How did Heurodis die?

# On the stage

Plays have been put on in theaters for thousands of years. On the stage, the actors play out dramas that may make the audience laugh or cry. The actors often wear costumes or paint their faces. They are lit up by stage lights. Some actors perform in public places such as schools or in the street, rather than in a theater. Dancers may appear on stage, too. They whirl or step in time to the music, or perform a graceful ballet. Opera is a play with songs instead of words.

opera

musical

street peformers

ballet

kabuki theater

▲ **Performance**

*Performers use various combinations of words, music, dance, and costumes to entertain their audience. Orchestras often provide the music.*

**act out**

Make up a short play with your friends and put on a show for your family. Or, you could act out a well-known story or fairytale.

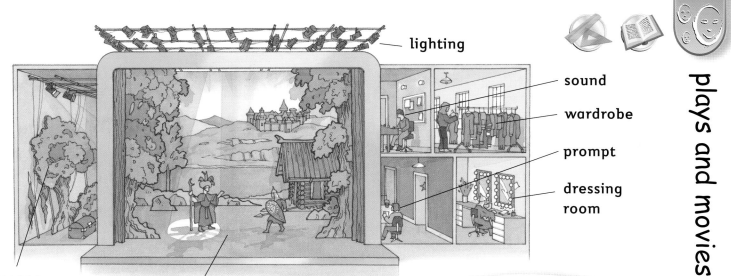

lighting

sound

wardrobe

prompt

dressing room

scenery

stage

### ▲ Putting on a play

*Lighting, sound effects, and scenery are all as much a part of a play as the acting.*

## What are shadow puppets?

Shadow puppets are popular in parts of Asia. A lamp casts shadows from the puppets onto a cotton screen. The shadows move kind of like figures in a movie. There are other kinds of puppet shows, too. Glove puppets are worked by hand, while marionettes are pulled by strings.

### ▲ Shakespeare's plays

*This actor is playing the character of Othello, in a play by William Shakespeare. This great writer lived in England between 1564 and 1616.*

### ▶ School stage

*Many famous actors started out performing in school plays like this one in the Caribbean.*

# Movies and television

**Lights, action!** In 1895 two French brothers named Louis and Auguste Lumière showed the first-ever moving pictures to the public. The first movies were in black and white only and had no sound. Today, we have big theaters and can also watch movies, shows, and news in our own homes, on color television or video.

▲ *Modern movies such as* Godzilla *(1998) use clever special effects.*

▶ **Television studio**
*Television programs are made in special indoor studios or outside in real places (on location). Strong lights and cameras are used to give clear, sharp pictures.*

▲ **Movie stars**
*Charlie Chaplin was born in England in 1889. He became one of the first world-famous film stars.*

India makes about 1,000 movies a year – more than any other country.

# Shakespeare
# and the Globe theater

**W**illiam Shakespeare was born in Stratford-upon-Avon, England in 1564, and died on the same date in 1616. He is probably the most well-known playwright in the world and his plays are still performed today.

Shakespeare left Stratford, probably in 1585, with a group of visiting London actors. In Tudor England, actors traveled the country performing at inns. They set up stage against a courtyard wall, and audiences watched from the ground or inn windows. In the later part of the 16th century, theaters began to be built, especially in London. By 1594 Shakespeare had written a number of plays, and he began to concentrate on his writing skills instead of his acting. He often based his plays on well-known stories and histories.

Shakespeare was a member of the Lord Chamberlain's Men, whose plays were performed at the theater in Shoreditch, London. In 1597 when James Burbage, the theater owner, died, it looked as if the theater would close. The Lord Chamberlain's Men and Burbage's sons decided to move the theater to the South Bank of the River Thames in London. They took every piece of timber and rebuilt the theater as the Globe. It opened in 1599 and was soon the most popular theater in London. It was a round building with a thatched roof and held audiences of almost 3,000 people, many of whom stood in the open air. Shakespeare wrote most of his greatest plays during his company's time at the Globe. It was during a performance of *Henry VIII,* in 1613, that the Globe burned down. A second Globe, built in 1614, was torn down in 1644. Work to reconstruct the Shakespeare's Globe theater started in 1993. It opened in 1997, 200 meters (660 feet) away from the site of the original Globe. It holds audiences of 2,080 people – 700 standing and 1,380 sitting.

A true story

When was William Shakespeare born? When did the Globe burn down?

# Can you remember?

Now that you have finished reading about people of the world, try answering the following questions. Each picture contains a clue – the page number where you will find the answer.

◀ **1** How did people use the Sun to tell the time?

▶ **2** Which civilization invented the wheel, and when?

▼ **3** Where did the Olmec people live?

▼ **4** Why should Egyptian school children have worshipped this god?

◀ **5** What were Japanese knights called?

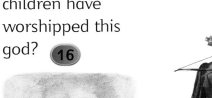

▶ **6** Which European explorer reached the Caribbean Sea in 1492?

▲ **7** Who flew the world's first plane?

▼ **8** What is a kayak?

▶ **9** Where is the Calgary Stampede held?

▼ **10** Where do people make boats from reeds? **44**

▼ **11** Can you name the different places where these people come from?

**54**

▼ **12** What did the Ancient Sumerians use instead of money? **57**

▼ **13** Why would you visit a lawyer's office?

**59**

**69**

▲ **14** In what country is the River Ganges?

**70**

◄ **15** Which people welcome in their New Year with a dragon?

**76**

► **16** What can you learn about a country by looking at its stamps? **73**

**81**

▲ **17** How often are the Olympic Games held?

▲ **18** What is this type of paint called?

► **19** What is a group of people who sing together called? **83**

► **20** Where was the first Globe theater?

**89**

# Index

This index is an alphabetical list of subjects contained within the pages of your book. Some of the subjects have another alphabetical list underneath them. These are called sub-entries, and they tell you what sort of information you can find about the main subject. The page numbers where you will find the most information are printed in **bold**.

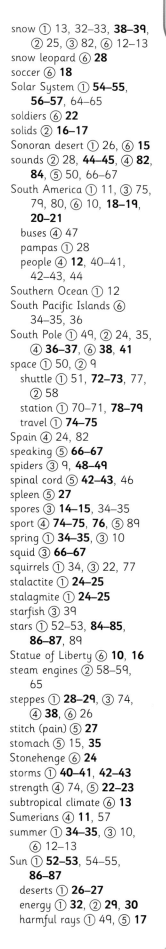

**The publishers would like to thank the following artists whose work appears in this book:** Kuo Kang Chen, Mike Foster/Maltings Partnership, Roger Goode/Beehive Illustration, Jeremy Gower, Peter Gregory, Ron Hayward, Rob Holder/Beehive Illustration, Rob Jakeway, Sue King/SGA, Janos Marffy, Tracey Morgan/BL Kearley Ltd, Jenny Press/SGA, GardnerQuainton, Terry Riley, Martin Sanders, Peter Sarson, Mike Saunders, Guy Smith/Mainline Design, Nick Spender/Advocate Ltd, Roger Stewart, Gwen Tourret/BL Kearley Ltd, Mike White/Temple Rogers.

**The publishers would like to thank the following sources for the use of their photographs in this book:** Robert Bosch Ltd: 61 (t/r). Corbis: 8 (b/c) Bettmann; 79 (c/r) Richard T. Nowitz; 8 (c/r) Galen Rowell; 12 (c/l) Gregor Schmid; 30 (c/l) John Wilkinson; 64 (t/r) Michael S. Yamashita. Early Learning Centre: 16 (b/r). Eurotunnel: 82 (b/r) QA Photos Ltd. Frank Lane Picture Agency: 39 (b/l) F. Polking. The Hutchison Library: 69 (c/r). Kenwood Ltd: 57 (t/l). Legoland: 17 (t/r). Skyscan: 55 (b/c) Austin J. Brown; 75 (b/l) GR Photography; 75 (b/r) Gavin Skipp. The Stock Market: 8 (b/r), 35 (b/l), 55 (b/r), 61 (b/l), 82 (c/l). All other photographs from Miles Kelly archives.
Abbreviations: t=top, b=bottom, c=centre, l=left, r=right